EMOTIONAL REGULATION SKILLS FOR **TEENS**

30+ ACTIVITIES TO CONQUER YOUR NEGATIVE THOUGHTS,

MANAGE EMOTIONS AND AGGRESSIVE BEHAVIOUR.

IMPROVE COPING SKILLS THROUGH CBT AND DBT.

BY

MARY J.

SERENE PUBLICATIONS

About the Author

Mary J. is a prominent dialectical and cognitive behavioral therapist and mental health specialist. Her works emphasize utilizing DBT and CBT techniques to assist people. She understands completely that teens can control their emotions and work to maintain long-term wellness. She has written several books for teens. "Emotional Regulation Skills Workbook for Teens" is one of her best teen books.

TABLE OF CONTENT

Introduction

Perhaps you have been feeling down a lot lately, you have observed yourself getting angry easily, or you have realized that you have been feeling nervous lately. This book's major objective is to teach you how to control your emotions as a teen so that you do not let them rule their actions and make mistakes you will later regret. Teen years are challenging.

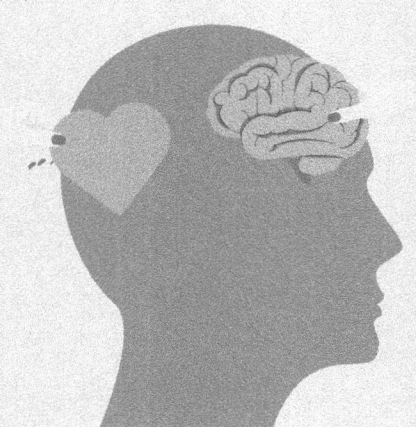

We all experience emotions; they are a vital component of our existence. Learning to control your emotions is becoming more conscious of how you feel and deciding what to do with them so that you do not injure yourself or other people. It entails learning to accept your feelings rather than trying to suppress them, especially when they are unpleasant.

Consider how you now handle your emotions. Do you allow yourself to feel them? Do you frequently lash out at those you care about when you are in agony and unsure of how to make yourself feel better? Or perhaps you try to mask your emotions and keep others from realizing how hurt you are inside by using humor.

Any methods you employ to attempt and suppress your emotions or learn to deal with how you are feeling are undoubtedly ineffective. You will learn the techniques you need to regulate your emotions in a healthy way from this book. You will notice that you will feel better about yourself and that your relationships will run more smoothly once you can do that.

When you take charge of your life, you will be able to lead a healthier and happier existence. Dr. Marsha Linehan developed dialectical behavior therapy (DBT) in 1993. She created this therapy to aid those who struggled greatly with emotion regulation. People with this kind of emotional issue frequently end up physically harming themselves, or at the very least, they engage in behaviors that actually worsen their lives.

You will learn the CBT and DBT techniques in this book to assist yourself in leading a healthier, less stressful life. You will acquire crucial knowledge about your emotions, which will enable you to better manage them and boost the positive emotions in your life. Your ability to cope with stress will enable you to avoid making matters worse and forging better connections with others.

Everyone is familiar with the idea that inspiration inspires action. The opposite is true if you are depressed: motivation comes from action. Or to put it another way, motivation and action go hand in hand like food and hunger. You eat because you are hungry. You keep alive through eating, and someday you will become hungry again. When someone is ill and does not feel like eating, they are frequently urged to eat anyhow because the food would help them regain their strength. You must start the cycle of motivation by acting even when you do not feel like it in order to feel motivated. Good luck!

CHAPTER 1

UNDERSTANDING EMOTIONS

In this chapter, you will discover some crucial things about emotions such as what emotions are, how they affect our behavior and why emotional regulation is important for you as a teen. You might discover that the difficulties you have managing your emotions are simply a result of the way you have been relating to them.

1.1. What Are Emotions?

Calling an emotion, a feeling is not completely correct even though feeling how you feel is undoubtedly a part of an emotion. To put it another way, an emotion entails not just how you feel, but also physical reactions (changes in body chemistry and body language), thoughts, and behaviors (including memories, images, and urges). For instance, you do not simply feel nervous; you also experience other things.

You experience anxious and negative thoughts (What if I cannot do this?) and the urge to act; with anxiety, this urge is frequently to run away to escape a situation or to avoid it in the first place. Your body language, including your facial expression, changes.

Some people frequently lack awareness of their emotions and appear to be in an "emotional fog." Do you try to block off your feelings and stop thinking about them? This frequently leads to emotional dysregulation, in part because people find it harder to control their emotions and feelings when they cannot give them a name or title. The next step is to learn to identify our emotions.

Basic Human Emotions

Understanding human emotions will help you improve your ability to name them over time, or alternatively, you will grow more assured that you can already do so.

Anger

Anger is an emotion, while aggression is a behavior that some individuals nearly always experience. If this describes you, you will notice that you get angry anytime something emotionally upsetting occurs. Hence, it is crucial to consider what are those circumstances that give rise to anger. These are a few instances:

When someone is disrespectful to you.

When there is a threat.

When you fail to accomplish a significant objective.

When you feel that you have been treated unfairly.

Adrenaline rushes in response to anger. It is a component of your body's fight-or-flight reaction, which prepares you to escape. As a result, you may have increased respiration and heart rate when you are angry. You feel heated, your muscles tense up, your breathing gets shallow, and you start to shake.

These are some phrases to characterize various forms of rage:

- Aggressive
- Annoyed
- Bitter
- Bothered
- Dissatisfied
- Enraged
- Exasperated
- Frustrated
- Furious
- Hostile
- Irritated
- Resentful

Fear

The fight-or-flight response that anger elicits is also brought on by fear, but fear is a little more nuanced since it may also bring on a freezing response that makes you feel nearly immobilized. Your muscles tense up and your respiration becomes shallow. Fear can also make you feel queasy or lightheaded, nauseated, and uncomfortable in your chest.

It can be challenging to identify which emotion you are experiencing because both anger and fear cause the same fight-or-flight response to be triggered.

Here are some scenarios when it would be reasonable to feel fear:

- When something or someone is posing a threat to you, such as when a stray dog approaches you.
- When a loved one is being harmed or threatened.
- When you fear losing someone or something significant to you.

These are some phrases to characterize various forms of fear:

- Afraid
- Alarmed
- Anxious
- Disconcerted
- Distraught
- Distressed
- Disturbed
- Frantic
- Nervous
- Overwhelmed
- Panicked
- Scared
- Stressed
- Tense
- Terrified
- Worried

Sadness

What does sadness physically feel like? You want to cry. It is also typical to feel exhausted or run-down, to have less energy than usual, or to feel drowsy. You might discover that you no longer like the things you used to enjoy doing and that you are left feeling hollow inside.

The desires that come with sadness frequently involve withdrawing from people and isolating yourself.

There are numerous causes of sadness. Here are several scenarios where you might experience sadness:

- When you lose a loved one, be it by death or the breakdown of a relationship.
- When you fail to achieve a significant objective (such as landing the dream job or getting accepted to the school of your dreams)
- When someone close to you is depressed or hurt.

These are some phrases to characterize various forms of sadness:

- Depressed
- Despairing
- Despondent
- Disheartened
- Distressed
- Dreary
- Forlorn
- Glum
- Grieving
- Heartbroken
- Hopeless
- Low
- Miserable
- Sorrowful
- Troubled
- Unhappy

Guilt or Shame

Let's first examine the distinction between guilt and shame. When you admit that you have done something wrong, you experience guilt. Shame, on the other hand, develops when you believe that whatever you did was wrong of you and that your behavior does not reflect well on you as a person. When you act in a way that goes against your principles and ideals, you condemn yourself for it and feel horrible about what you did.

Here are some instances where it would be appropriate to experience guilt or shame:

- When you engage in behavior that is contrary to your ethics and principles, such as lying or using a cheat sheet for an exam.
- When you receive criticism in public.
- When you recall or are reminded of an immoral act you formerly committed.
- When you do something, you believe is good for a group endeavor and get feedback indicating you shouldn't have done it.

Here are some phrases to describe various forms of remorse or shame:

- Apologetic
- Ashamed
- Blamed
- Degraded
- Disgraced
- Embarrassed
- Guilty
- Humiliated
- Mortified
- Regretful
- Remorseful
- Repentant

- Self-conscious
- Self-disgusted
- Sorry

Love

You probably feel more good emotions overall when you are in a loving relationship. You experience increased enjoyment of life, excitement at se (or animal), security, relaxation, and calm.

In the following circumstances, love is probably going to come into play:

- When you fall in love with someone because you are emotionally and physically drawn to them.
- When you witness their pride when you succeed at anything.

Here are some phrases to characterize various forms of love:

- Accepted
- Adoring
- Affectionate
- Attraction
- Caring
- Cherishing
- Connected
- Desiring
- Devoted
- Fondness
- Infatuated
- Love-struck

Happiness

When you are joyful, you want to grin and spread your joy to others. The impulses that come along with happiness vary depending on what you are glad about. For example, you might want to embrace someone you are happy to see, or if you have just learned something exciting, you might want to phone people you care about to let them know. Those who are happier tend to be more social and active.

But when it comes to happiness, we frequently have irrational expectations. Individuals frequently think that they "should" be happy and frequently wonder why they aren't. According to my observations, the majority of people do not spend their lives in a state of happiness. We may feel comfortable with our lives, satisfied, or at peace, but I do not believe that feelings of happiness stay for very long.

These are some phrases to characterize various forms of happiness:

- Amused
- Content
- Delighted
- Ecstatic
- Elated
- Glad
- Joyful
- Peaceful
- Pleased
- Proud
- Relaxed
- Relieved
- Satisfied
- Serene

I hope you have completely grasped basic human emotions. Let's move forward.

1.2. How do Emotions Affect Behavior?

When we experience an emotion, we have specific thoughts and we act according to that emotion. People frequently conflate thoughts and acts with actual emotions as a result of this.

Altering one's emotions will alter their thoughts and behaviors, altering one's thoughts will alter their behaviors and emotions, and altering one's behaviors will alter their emotions and thoughts. It is really simple to mix up these three sectors because they are so closely related.

It is crucial to learn to keep your emotions distinct from your behaviors and thoughts. Your task now is to distinguish between what you are feeling (do not forget to refer back to the list of emotions if necessary) and what you are thinking, as well as how you are behaving (not what you felt like doing or wanted to do, but the actions you actually took).

It is becoming dark as you make your way home alone from your friend's place when you hear a disturbance. You might have an experience similar to this:

- ☐ Oh my God, what was that? (thought).
- ☐ While you scan the area to judge the circumstances (behavior).
- ☐ You notice strangers following you. "I've got a follower. What if I am attacked by them?" (thought).
- ☐ You sense fear (emotion).
- ☐ Never will I be able to repel them. There is no one nearby to assist me (thought).
- ☐ Your terror level rises (emotion).
- ☐ You feel the want to flee the situation, so you think about your options (thought).
- ☐ You jog back to your friend's house by turning around and returning the way you came (behavior).

Let's now take a look at how altering just one part of your experience could alter this scenario.

It is becoming dark as you make your way home alone when you hear a disturbance.

- ☐ "What was that?" is what you initially think. (thought).
- ☐ You scan the area to judge the circumstances (behavior).
- ☐ You notice strangers following you. They do not appear recognizable (thought).
- ☐ You are intrigued (emotion).
- ☐ You keep watching them (behavior).
- ☐ Noting that there are three teenage girls in the group (thought).
- ☐ You reflect about what you ought to do (thought).
- ☐ You are a little worried about them because it is becoming dark outside (emotion).
- ☐ You approach and inquire if they require assistance navigating (behavior).

Thus, using the identical initial scenario as a starting point, here are two completely different results.

1.3. The Importance of Emotional Regulation

We'll then continue to work on altering the way you see your emotions by examining the purpose they serve. Or, to put it another way, what do they do? Certainly, despite how unpleasant circumstances are and how much you might want to throw your emotions out the window, they do serve a function, and we do need them. Only then, we will be able to regulate them. There are some explanations for why we feel emotions.

- The first is that your emotions inspire you to act or compel you to do something. Consider bullying as an illustration. When students witness bullying behaviors, they may become inspired to act and protest in some way. Fear can inspire action as well. Your fight-or-flight reaction prepares you to either stand and fight or flee the situation when your brain detects something that could be a threat to you. In any case, the emotion serves as inspiration and inspires you to act in some way.

- Emotions can also inform you of a scenario you want to alter in order to make it more in line with your requirements or desires. Again, in this case, your anger may have made you realize that there is something about the situation that is unfair or that you dislike for another reason; alternatively, your guilt makes you realize that you are acting in a way that is inconsistent with your principles and beliefs.

- The final function of emotions is to improve your ability to communicate with others. Others around you may frequently infer how you are feeling based only on your facial expression and behavior. It is because emotions are linked to distinct facial expressions and body language, making it easy for us to recognize them in ourselves and others. They'll be able to estimate what you are feeling very correctly if you start crying or start clenching your jaw and reddening your face.

Although your emotions have a function, it is crucial to understand that they are fallible and shouldn't be taken as fact. You must assess something before accepting it just because of how you feel. While trying a new dish, you are frequently wary about it and test to check if your sense of smell is accurate because just because something smells nice does not necessarily mean it tastes good.

It is crucial to keep in mind that while your emotions do have a function, they do not always do it well. Changing your relationship with your emotions is one of our objectives here. They've undoubtedly caused you a lot of trouble up to this point since they may be frightening and painful, and they can have a lot of unfavorable effects when you are riding the emotional roller coaster.

Therefore, consider emotions as just another sense. Your emotions are just another sense like sight that you have to help you learn and make decisions. How does your vision fare? Without it, life would be challenging. Thus, try your best not to judge your emotions and instead think of them as just another sense that is giving you information.

To put all the knowledge, you have gained, we will now do some activities. You can ensure that you have a solid base upon which to develop as you progress through this book.

1.4. Activity Corner

It is your turn to do some fun part and learn.

Activity 1: What does Your Emotions Do?

You have learned what kind of emotions do we have and how our emotions serve a purpose. After reading the story below, respond to the questions.

Anne's father had recently remarried, and her parents had divorced when she was twelve. His new wife frequently criticized Anne and seemed to be trying to act as Anne's mother, which Anne didn't appreciate. Anne once visited her father to see him after school. She was pleased with herself for her grade in arithmetic because it was a subject she had always found difficult. Before her father could see Anne's report card, his new wife glanced at it and warned the girl that her Bs were unacceptable and that she would need to work much more.

Mark the feeling that most accurately sums up how Anne might be feeling.

Anger   Sadness   Anxiety   Guilt

What function might this emotion serve?

_____

_____

What action might Anne undertake as a result of this feeling?

_____

_____

Can you think of a time when you have had each of these feelings? Spend some time thinking about the purpose it served and the things you performed as a result, then share your thoughts in the area provided:

When I was angry:

_____

_____

This emotion's function is:

_____

_____

What I did that was beneficial:

_____

_____

Activity 2: Identify the Triangle

Identify the Triangle

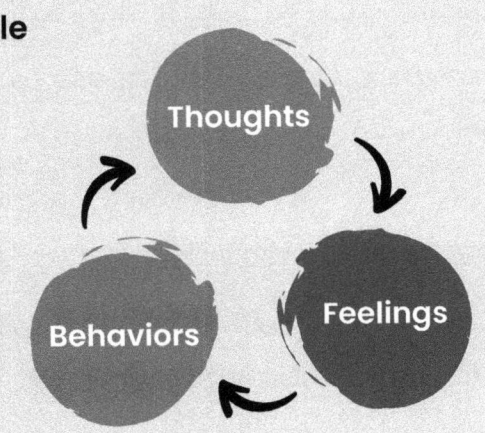

You now understand how your emotions, thoughts, and actions are related. Put that knowledge to use right away. The phrase that most accurately sums up each one of them in each statement should be written in front of it.

I hate school.

_____

I am worried about taking my exams the following week.

_____

I complete my homework.

_____

My parents and I argue.

_____

Never will I be in a relationship.

_____

I regret missing the concert.

_____

My new dog is amazing.

_____

My sister turned down my request to play with her, which makes me sad.

_____

You might not be able to tell this triangle apart right away. The majority of people are not used to needing to think in this way, so do not worry if you struggle with some of these.

But you must concentrate on this since it will help you have more control over them.

Activity 3: Acceptance Sets You Free

Accepting that painful events have occurred or are now occurring in our lives can be challenging. Hence, we choose to battle reality rather than accepting it. But, when we reject these realities, there is no doubt that the reality of the occurrences remains unchanged. Avoiding reality does not make things better; on the contrary, it only makes us feel worse.

You need to accept reality and act appropriately rather than resisting it and trying to change it into something it is not.

Recall one of the circumstances that you still find difficult to accept.

What could you tell yourself to make you more receptive to this circumstance?

_____

_____

_____

_____

_____

_____

_____

_____

CHAPTER 2

WHAT ARE NEGATIVE THOUGHTS?

Let's understand negative thoughts now that you know what emotions are and how they affect your behavior. Your brain considers all factors, not just potential threats. Additionally, your heart is being heard. You are aware deep down that life is about more than just surviving. Your aspirations for the future and your ideal way of living are held within your heart.

The fundamental tenet of this book is to help you have a better chance of regaining control of your life by becoming more adept at distinguishing between what is real and what is not. In this chapter, you will learn to identify your negative thoughts and their origins. You will learn how you become conscious of how these thoughts feed your anxious mind.

2.1. The Diet of an Anxious Mind

Let's see what your anxious mind eats.

The Wild Guesses of Oliver's Anxious Mind

Oliver, who was fifteen, adored cycling. He went to his friend's place and made the most of his time. One day, while he returned home from cycling with his friend, a park's off-leash dog started pursuing him. Oliver didn't hear the dog approaching since he listened to music through headphones. He was thrown off his cycle when the dog pursued him and caught up to him. The dog's owner promptly emerged and removed the dog while profusely apologizing. Although Oliver wasn't bitten, he felt like he might have been. While he walked home injured and shaken, he assured the dog's owner he was fine.

The following day, Oliver was cycling. He saw a neighbor walking her big dog and heading straight toward him. Similar to how he had felt the day before, he noticed that his heart was starting to beat rapidly and that he was experiencing terror. He returned to his home and felt a lot calmer as soon as he entered.

Oliver remained calm by avoiding dogs, but this did not make him less afraid of them. He only needed to consider cycling to become uncomfortable around dogs. Avoidance exacerbated his anxiety and prevented him from engaging in activities he enjoyed.

Your belief that your action has stopped something horrible from happening is why your anxiety worsens. Oliver was relieved and noticed that he was inside his home and the dog had not bitten him.

You may wonder why he would continue to think like that. Do you ever pause or consider something more carefully before sounding your alarms and get panicked? No. The sole purpose of your anxious mind is to keep you secure. Also, your mind becomes hyperactive and reactive to danger if you have anxiety. It is unable to distinguish between imagined and actual threats. Its fearful ideas are just wild conjectures, not thoroughly reasoned concepts.

You essentially accept that the scenario was unsafe when you avoided it out of anxiety. You are teaching your mind to read things the same way, babble the same way, and raise the alarm the next time.

You might not realize that what you are doing is an avoidance tactic. You search for a solution to a problem by thinking about it repeatedly in your head to stop feeling nervous. You are trying to keep yourself from experiencing the anxiety the issue causes.

Oliver's mind made some wild guesses, so it is crucial to understand the diet of your anxious mind.

The Spice of Overestimation

When assessing risk, your anxious mind continuously commits two errors: it overestimates the likelihood that something negative will occur, and it underestimates the likelihood that something good will occur. It undervalues your capacity to handle difficult situations. This double error interprets safe circumstances as dangerous, triggering false alarms and your body's fight-or-flight response.

The Worst Leap

The most typical error is catastrophizing or jumping to the worst-case scenario. The anxious mind constantly imagines the worst-case scenario, like in a scary movie. Following are a few illustrations of the worst leaps:

- You are not raising your hand in class to respond to a question. If you do this incorrectly, a rumor about your stupidity will spread among the students.
- Your chest is constricting. Are you having a heart attack?
- You need help with a test. If you fail this, you won't be admitted to college, and it will appear on your transcript.

Ask your anxious mind, "What's likely to happen?"

The Salt of Negativity

Every event we face has both positive and negative components, but because the anxious mind is constantly scanning for threats, it entirely ignores the positive aspects of our experiences and adds the salt of the negativity. This is what we mean when we devalue the good. For example, you receive an English paperback with encouraging remarks. But your focus is drawn to one area that could immediately be improved. You think that you are a hopeless writer!

The Soup of Mind Reading

Your anxious mind makes assumptions about what other people are thinking about you.

- You have a fresh hairstyle as you move down the corridor. Everyone is gazing at your hair!
- You are dining by yourself in a sandwich shop. You do not seem to have any pals.
- Ask yourself, "What evidence do I have that people are thinking about you?" if you believe you can read minds.

A Perfect Recipe

You believe that you must consistently deliver faultless performance. Anything less is not acceptable and will expose you to risk and criticism. The anxious mind concurs. It wants a perfect recipe. Consider this: "Do I have higher expectations for myself?"

Let's move on to some activities to grasp what we have learned in this chapter.

2.2. Activity Corner

Here comes the fun and interesting part.

Activity 4: Identify Your Anxious Mind

To control your anxious mind, first, it is essential to identify it.

Check the options that apply to you.

- ☐ You experience worry when you are apart from your loved ones.
- ☐ You suddenly become afraid when you are in a vehicle, an aircraft, a bridge, or a confined space.
- ☐ You frequently ruminate about your following words or actions before engaging in social interactions.
- ☐ You suddenly experience weird or distant feelings or a false sense of reality.
- ☐ You experience anxiety, nervousness, or worry around others, in public areas, on public transit, or when you are distant from home.
- ☐ You frequently worry about unfavorable events like accidents, tragedies in your family, or illness.
- ☐ You double-check everything to make sure nothing negative occurs.
- ☐ Some animals or insects make you feel anxious.
- ☐ You need help speaking up in class.
- ☐ You worry that a panic attack will cause you to lose control, pass away, go insane, or experience other unfavorable events.
- ☐ You worry about having panic attacks, experiencing unpleasant bodily sensations or experiencing overwhelming anxiety when you are in a crowded place, on a solo trip, or away from home.
- ☐ You fret over receiving poor grades or getting into trouble at school.
- ☐ Do storms, heights, or water make you nervous?

- ☐ In an unexpected event, you occasionally experience symptoms like a beating heart, sweating, difficulty breathing, dizziness, or shakiness.
- ☐ You stay near exits when using public transit or in locations like schools and movie theaters.
- ☐ You frequently feel tight and restless or struggle to unwind or fall asleep.
- ☐ You get fear or dizziness when you see blood or needles.
- ☐ You find it incredibly awkward to initiate or join a conversation.
- ☐ You avoid being in circumstances where you can feel imprisoned, sung a car passenger or in a line.
- ☐ You struggle to focus as a result of worry and anxiety.
- ☐ You experience distress from impermissible religious or sexual thoughts.
- ☐ You worry that you will choke up.
- ☐ You refrain from making outbound calls or texts to someone you do not know well.
- ☐ You worry or have anxiety about having other panic attacks.
- ☐ You frequently have headaches or stomachaches.
- ☐ You must say something or do something several times before it seems fitting.
- ☐ You experience anxious thoughts that make you want to hurt yourself or someone else.

Go over the statements you checked off. Your likelihood of experiencing worry and anxiety increases with the number of checkmarks you have.

Activity 5: Spot Your Negative Thoughts

Grab your negative thoughts. Think about a situation when you feel anxious and answer the following question.

What are you afraid of?

_____

_____

_____

What would be the worst scenario if this came to pass?

_____

_____

_____

What does this mean for you, your life, and your prospects?

_____

_____

_____

Activity 6: Challenging Your Anxious Thoughts

Remember the worst leap we talked about in this chapter? Well! Time to face that. After identifying and spotting your anxious and negative thoughts, it is crucial to challenge them. Thinking about the same situation you imagined in the previous activity, challenge your anxious thoughts with the following questions.

What is likely to occur?

_____

_____

What went well? What was the right thing that I did?

_____

_____

Do I hold myself to higher standards than I would hold others?

_____

_____

What will I lose by having no risk in my life?

_____

Activity 7: What are You Avoiding?

Your anxious mind wants to give you a perfect diet and keep your away from beautiful things by instructing you to avoid them. It is time to be honest with yourself and face your anxious mind with courage.

What do you believe your fear is preventing you from doing?

What activities did you once enjoy but no longer do?

What are you avoiding?

_____

_____

_____

_____

_____

_____

CHAPTER 3

CBT COPING SKILLS TO CONQUER NEGATIVE THOUGHTS

Becoming a recently licensed driver made James incredibly happy. A week after gaining his independence, a horrible accident occurred near his home where a teen ran down and killed a person crossing the street. The next time James was driving, he felt a slight jolt in the pavement. He had the feeling that perhaps he had just run over someone. He knew this was absurd, but he could not shake the worry. Even though he looked in his rearview mirror and saw nothing, he was still tense. His uneasiness didn't go away until he returned to the location where he'd felt the bump and realized nothing was there.

If you experience thoughts like James, then CBT can help you.

The widely used and successful Cognitive Behavioral Therapy (CBT) method can be used to treat and manage various mental health problems. CBT stresses the relationship between a person's ideas, feelings, and behaviors and teaches them how to identify and question any opposing thoughts or beliefs that might upset them. This chapter will examine how CBT can assist people in overcoming negative beliefs.

By helping people recognize their negative automatic thoughts—quick, reflexive responses that happen in response to particular situations or events—CBT combats negative thinking. CBT will assist you in challenging these negative habitual thoughts and replacing them with more reasonable and balanced ones using a variety of exercises and strategies.

3.1. Introduction to CBT

Cognitive behavioral therapy (CBT) can assist individuals in examining the various contexts in which they find themselves and comprehending their ideas, bodily sensations, and behavioral patterns. The theory is that our behaviors, thoughts, and feelings may all interact with one another and support the maintenance of negative emotions like depression and anxiety. Look at the illustration below.

According to cognitive behavioral therapy (CBT), an individual's emotional distress is often caused by how they interpret or see a situation rather than by the circumstance itself. CBT involves learning how to question harmful beliefs and alter unhelpful behaviors.

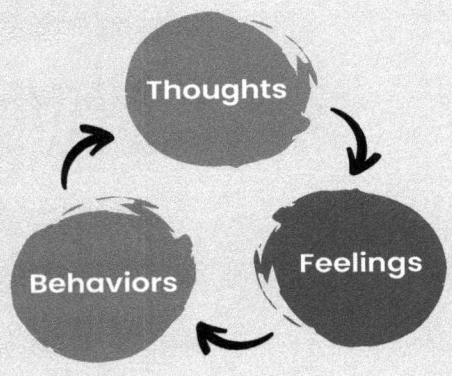

Negative automatic thoughts are frequent when we are depressed or stressed. These negative ideas automatically cross our minds and are not beneficial. Although it may temporarily lessen their worry, it can reinforce and maintain it over time. Stopping this loop may initially make you feel more anxious but will ultimately help you feel less anxious.

As an illustration, consider Emily, who gets anxious when she goes to the store. She feels feverish, her heart is racing, and she has trouble breathing. She believes, "I am suffering a heart attack," which worsens her physical problems. As a result, she tries to get away from them as quickly as possible.

When she reencounters this situation, it can make Emily feel even more apprehensive, and it might also reinforce her negative ideas. Her feelings, symptoms, and behaviors are all affected by one another.

Emily Visiting a Store:

Her thought: I am experiencing a heart attack.

Her Behavior: Avoids the stores or refuses to enter them completely.

Her feeling: I am feeling low and anxious.

Negative thoughts are about a person's capacity to cope with fear, which can keep anxiety at bay. People occasionally develop coping skills that enable them to handle a problem. This can entail avoiding the circumstance or acting differently to assist them in managing their fear.

3.2. Challenging Your Negative Thoughts

Your anxiety and bad mood can be controlled by learning to control your negative thoughts. Teens frequently have extreme or irrational thoughts when depressed or anxious. These thoughts are known as negative automatic thoughts in cognitive behavioral therapy (CBT).

These are the kinds of ideas that would make anyone uncomfortable. Although some people recognize that their negative ideas are not genuine, doing so can be challenging for people who are anxious or in a bad mood. Therefore, these individuals frequently believe their negative thoughts to be true. Hence, this kind of negative thinking might keep us in a depressed or anxious state.

How can Thinking Critically Benefit You?

The purpose of this strategy is to examine reasonable and balanced manner rather than merely focusing on the positive aspects of them. Your attitude and ability to perform will be enhanced by more balanced ideas, allowing you to resume enjoying life.

At first, you will need to allow the procedures, but with practice, you will be able to employ this strategy throughout a challenging event to lift your spirits at the time.

How This Method Operates

Our thoughts are frequently shaped by our opinions and experiences rather than objective reality. When we are depressed or nervous, our thoughts also have a negative tilt. This can cause us to make hasty assumptions or imagine the worst-case scenario without supporting data.

We need to gather information while addressing negative thoughts to see how true they are. Because there is no room for doubt, factual evidence is significantly more persuasive than opinion.

The objective is to examine the belief that generates the most emotional anguish to determine its degree of reality. We then formulate a fresh, evidence-based alternative idea.

What Distinguishes a Thinking from an Emotion?

Often, thoughts consist of a sentence or a claim about something or someone. A single word that sums up how we feel is an emotion.

Thoughts like "Nobody likes me" are examples. "People think I am foolish" "If I am late for work, I'll lose my job."

A few examples of emotions are anger, happiness, anxiety, and depression as discussed in chapter 1.

Seeking an Alternative or Evidence-Based Thinking

Cognitive restructuring consists of three steps:

First Step: Gathering Thoughts

Choose a circumstance that made you feel unfavorable emotions to start.

Write out specifics about the circumstance first. Even if the circumstance may not have been the root of your unpleasant thoughts or feelings, jotting down specifics will help.

Next, try to pinpoint the "negative thought" in the circumstance. The likelihood that this concept would result in negative emotion is frequently regarded as the highest.

Because it is frequently something we are not accustomed to doing, stopping these thoughts can be challenging. You should repeat this first stage a few times as a result.

Asking yourself the following types of questions will assist you in clearing your mind.

- Who or what were you? How did you justify yourself?
- What was the worst thought that crossed your mind?

Asking yourself the following types of questions will assist you in clearing your mind.

- They are brief and precise.
- They happen immediately following the occurrence.
- They may appear as text or pictures.
- At the time, they seem sensible.
- They do not result from severe consideration or a logical progression of stages.

Step Two: Locating the Proof

Note the supporting and opposing arguments for what is happening. You are just interested in facts, not opinions. Imagine yourself as the prosecution and defense attorneys at a court hearing. Both sides will present evidence to uncover the truth.

You might want to ask yourself questions such as, "If my buddy or someone else was thinking this way, what would I say to them?"

How would I view the scenario if I weren't fearful or depressed?

Is there another angle from which to view the circumstances?

Thinking critically is similar to sitting in judgment on your case. The accused is your default negative thinking, such as "Everyone hates me." How trustworthy and solid is the evidence presented to back this? Is the statement, "Everyone hates me? I simply know it," sufficient proof?

Think about all the evidence, then use an alternate idea supported by the evidence to reach your conclusion.

Step Three: Seeking an Alternative or Evidence-Based Thinking

Lastly, you must formulate a fresh alternative idea using the facts gathered during Step two as a foundation. Instead of trying to think positively, this is trying to think more equitably, considering both arguments.

Write a statement summarizing the "evidence for" and another sentence summarizing the "evidence against" to develop an evidence-based thought.

Reevaluate your initial feelings in light of your revised (balanced) thinking. The purpose of this strategy is to lessen the intensity of your negative feelings.

An Overview of the Method

Here are the steps to challenge your negative thoughts:

1. Describe a circumstance in which you had a particularly unpleasant emotional state (such as anxiety or depression).
2. Name the feeling (e.g., depressed, anxious, low, sad).
3. Indicate how strong the emotion was.
4. List the negative thoughts that were occupying your thoughts at the time.
5. Indicate how much you truly believed the thoughts to be true.
6. Find your "negative thought." The only idea we will contest is the one that makes you feel the most emotional pain.
7. Find data that support your belief.
8. Find facts that contradict the viewpoint.
9. After the evidence supporting and refuting an idea has been gathered, reevaluate your position in light of the facts.
10. Combine the data obtained in stage 3 with "and," "or," and "but."
11. Make a more reasonable assessment.

The activities below will help you understand CBT skills and how they help in emotional regulation.

3.3. Activity Corner

Here is the fun and learning part.

Activity 8: Breath Your Anxiety

Imagine drawing strength from the earth with each breath, like the tree's roots. Each time you exhale, you relinquish control over the situation, swaying with the wind like a tree and accepting whatever occurs—including the possible worry it causes.

Fear can be overcome and softened by breathing into it. Your body begins to breathe shallowly in response to your anxious mind alarm, but you can change it with your slow, deep breaths.

Here's your turn:

Imagine yourself on a calm beach or another relaxing location till your nervousness subsides. That's escaping the circumstance. You must be present to accomplish your aim, like practicing mindfulness and fully experiencing each moment.

Do not try to change anything; allow everything to be as it is.

Breathe into any areas of your body that are tense. Do this for ten minutes, paying great attention to your body's experiences.

You will notice that your level of anxiety is shifting. Taking a breath will lower your resistance to anxiety and let it have its course of nature.

You are more powerful than your mind believes!

Activity 9: Keep Your Record

You must consider outcomes to make precise forecasts about the future. You can gather and assess information. Instead of depending on your mind's hunches, you may figure out how likely something will disturb you.

Record every time you have negative thoughts, including what you were thinking and what transpired.

Keep Your Record

Review this log after a week to determine how things stand.

Date	Your pessimistic attitude	Your mental forecast	What truly took place?

Activity 10: Look at Things Objectively

Why not examine the reason that is causing the worry critically before you spend more time worrying about it? You can determine whether you have a real threat or just another notion by considering both the evidence that the thought is accurate or not.

Here is a "Proof for and Against" response to the possibility that receiving a B grade may prevent you from being admitted to a prestigious university and leave you homeless.

Proof: It is accurate that you scored a B. Test scores impact overall class grades.

Proof Against: This test only accounted for 20% of your final class grade. While you currently have an A average in the class, this B will only affect your final grade if you receive a B or below on the upcoming test.

Alternative View: Although test scores can influence final grades, you would need to do poorly going forward to receive a failing mark in the class. You can enter many reputable institutions even if your final grade is a B.

Make sure to keep to the facts when using this tool. This is simply a potential future event; it is not a fact. Sometimes, sticking to the facts necessitates gathering more data.

Think about a situation and repeat this process and record your responses below:

_____

_____

_____

_____

_____

Activity 11: The Blue Sky

The body can experience a lot of tension. It provokes a fight-or-flight reaction. Your heart beats more quickly, your stomach stops digesting, and your muscles tense up so that more energy can be used. Here is what you need to do.

- You must sit or lie with no movement to complete this exercise.
- Go somewhere private, and switch off your phone.
- Start by taking deep, slow breaths.
- Repeat ten times.
- Now, look at the blue sky.
- Opens up and drips its blue contents down softly over you.
- It could be beneficial to play some music while doing this activity.
- You must follow these steps to observe the benefit of this relaxing approach.

Activity 12: Take Action

There is an additional reward for overcoming obstacles, melancholy and worry. The key is understanding how to increase your motivation by doing what you love to do. Your life will benefit significantly from action because nothing exists without it.

- Choose a new interest or activity to engage in.
- Something you need more motivation to undertake.
- It might be an exercise such as walking, riding a bike, dancing, or painting.
- No matter how drained or unmotivated you are, do that for five minutes daily.

You have all your life to achieve your goals and travel to your desired destinations. So why are you still waiting? It is time to go forward!

Activity 13: Who are Those People?

Below is a selection of typical scenarios that many teenagers having social anxiety find incredibly unsettling. Does any of them resonate with you?

- ☐ Having chats or continuing them
- ☐ Responding to inquiries in class
- ☐ Making a date request
- ☐ Asking a teacher for advice or assistance
- ☐ Participating in celebrations and events
- ☐ Blushing, trembling, sweating, or displaying other anxious symptoms
- ☐ Consuming food or writing in public
- ☐ Requesting a buddy to attend a gathering
- ☐ Performing for an audience

Now, answer the following questions:

Who are those people you have been keeping away from? Give each person a scariness score between 1 and 10, with ten being the most frightful.

_____

_____

_____

_____

What are you going to tell them?

_____

_____

_____

_____

A realistic objective is one that you can accomplish, given your abilities, timescale, and level of motivation. Yet you will come closer to reaching these objectives once you decide what they are.

Do you have any realistic goals that are worthy of a fight? If so, fill these stairs with them. Regaining control of your life can be done effectively by facing your anxieties and altering your behavior. But it takes work.

Activity 15: Cherish the Present Moment

The anxious and negative mind always looks back to see if you made any blunders. It keeps an eye out for danger by scanning the horizon. Of course, this causes anxiety. We may detach ourselves from all this and genuinely feel relief by concentrating on the here and now.

Do this:

- ☐ Take a moment to appreciate how the book feels in your hands.
- ☐ Take note of your seating or sleeping arrangements.
- ☐ Become conscious of the current sounds or stillness in the space.
- ☐ Anytime you brush your teeth, shower, or eat a mouthful of cereal, you may practice paying attention.
- ☐ Try looking closely at the nearby people, trees, and buildings while walking along the street.

You will be astounded by what you discover. Take a moment to write what you felt.

_____

_____

_____

_____

_____

_____

CHAPTER 4

UNDERSTANDING YOUR ANGER AND AGGRESSIVE BEHAVIOR

Tom had a bad attitude. He used to engage in conflict at school. He had a few pals who were like him. Most of the time, they just caused trouble. Tom frequently got into problems and faced harsh criticism from teachers and the principal. Tom had been contaminated by the seeds of aggression, which grew with time.

Tom behaved politely, quietly, and respectfully at home. At least, that was how it appeared. He heard his parents arguing all the time loudly. His older brother endured much verbal and physical abuse from their father. Tom constantly felt as though he was physically or verbally attacked. Tom frequently got upset with his abusive and cruel father. He disliked his mother for continuing to be around and endure the abuse. For his brother, he was terrified. Tom felt helpless in the face of their father's strict rule over the household. Tom could let some of this rage out at school, so he did.

Do you have that seed of anger?

You weren't bred to be angry. Nobody among us was. Aggression, though, is all around us. Anger may act as a seed that grows within us. What was once imposed upon us may develop within comes a part of who we are.

Have you ever wondered why you lash out so much? Where did this anger originate? Why are you unable to restrain yourself? Ask yourself some of these questions. Anger is a strong and sophisticated emotion. The roots of rage can be pretty deep and stretch out in many ways. This chapter will discuss some factors contributing to anger and aggressiveness while also challenging you to look into the sources of your rage.

4.1. Anger: A Strong Emotion

People typically have issues with your actions rather than your feelings. Because everyone focuses on getting you to stop doing what you do—arguing, fighting, or engaging in aggressive behavior—so many anger-management techniques fail. People would likely be more understanding if they knew why you did something, but no one always has that information.

Why do emotions like contentment or tranquility seem weaker in our bodies than anger and fear? It is because they trigger the fight-or-flight reaction, which is an emergency alarm system. Our bodies immediately strive to defend ourselves when we detect danger, which gives us an energy boost. We develop heightened environmental awareness. Our more sophisticated brain processes turn off as our bodies prepare for action.

This response is crucial when there is a genuine threat to our survival. We have to act quickly in certain situations. We respond without fully considering the best course of action. Often, our anger is covered by an emotion called fear. You may suppress or cover up a variety of worries with your fury. Even if they do not threaten your physical safety, your mental anxieties could hinder your fight-or-flight response.

Real threats usually prevent fights from breaking out. Humans tend to perceive danger and risks everywhere. Our emotions can become dominated by anger and hatred, which feeds into a vicious cycle of fury that is challenging to break. A self-fulfilling prophecy is referred to as when a pattern causes us to create a reality that reflects how we perceive ourselves and other people. The world will become violent around you if your attention is on being angry.

4.2. How does Anger Operate?

Let's understand how your anger operates using Tom's story:

Negative self-view is the negative self-talk we frequently pick up from others.

Tom believed that everyone hated him.

An outside trigger is anything that occurs and sets off our reactions.

A classmate unintentionally bumped Tom during school.

An internal trigger is a strong negative emotional response to the incident. Tom believed that he was playing a joke on him.

Due to an outburst of rage, Tom shoved a classmate in the face and knocked him into the lockers.

Adults will likely respond with rejection, disappointment, and punishment.

Tom's parents scolded him and had him suspended from school.

Rejection, anxiety, and avoidance from peers act as a response.

Tom's peers avoided him as they believed he was cruel and uncontrollable.

Reality starts to confirm the negative self-view, creating a self-fulfilling prophecy.

As evidence that everyone despised him, Tom used to show aggressive behavior.

Power Conflicts

How frequently do you feel that everyone is out to get you? Power conflicts are one of the main reasons why people get angry and aggressive and are also a significant reason why children and their parents argue. Power has many effects on anger management issues.

You may feel helpless, for instance, when you have little control. Being an adolescent and wanting to make your own life, all these rules and regulations might feel like curse.

A constant sense of helplessness may encourage anger.

Another illustration of abuse of power is using force to exert control over others. You might abuse authority because you feel helpless in one area of your life. It is a means of getting even with the person who made you feel bad.

Habits of aggressive behavior frequently result from unhealthy power struggles. Perhaps your parents or friends taught you that putting others in danger will help you get what you want. The prospect of out-of-control behavior, such as violence or meltdowns, may help you keep your parents under control. But is this the kind of connection you want?

Others, including teachers and friends, might wait to give in. They may even steer clear of you. Power abuse can offer you authority over others in the short term. That will ultimately make you misuse empowerment. You do not feel helpless, and you do not abuse your influence over other people. Instead, you possess a strong self-confidence that allows you to accomplish your goals without harming others.

4.3 Activity Corner

Activity 16: Identify Your Anger Pattern

Think about a situation when you were angry. Answer the questions given below.

What was the trigger (your problem)?

_____

_____

Your thoughts:

_____

_____

Your feelings:

_____

_____

Your behavior:

_____

_____

Consequences:

_____

_____

A Mindful Action

Take the following steps if you notice that you are going to act aggressively. Consider a circumstance that makes you angry, then fill in the blanks with your replies.

Pause: Do not do it

_____

_____

Tell yourself: "Think"

_____

_____

Take action: What to do in its place

_____

_____

Improve Your Self-Talk

Here are some suggestions for positive self-talk. Which ones you pick to control your rage is entirely up to you. What would you pick from them?

- ☐ I would not permit them to hurt me in any way.
- ☐ They never heed my recommendations. That is not right but it is okay if they do not get me.
- ☐ I know I can fix this problem.
- ☐ I can control my anger.
- ☐ I am lucky.
- ☐ I will rise again.

Activity 19: Conflict Resolution

The definition of conflict resolution includes mutual ownership and "we have a problem."

Here is an example of what it means and how we can do conflict resolution.

Have current & forward-looking: "maybe the next time we..."

The problem seems to be: "the issue seems to be..."

"It sounds like we agree on the problem," is the agreed-upon issue.

Have resolution to the problem: listen (observe, acknowledge, do not interrupt), check out, and say, "let me see if I understand..."

"I can imagine how you would feel that way," you say.

Let's brainstorm all the options that might be available.

"I would appreciate it if..." is a positive presentation.

Do compromise: "sounds like we have agreed to try..."

"Let me make sure that I comprehend the terms we've agreed to," you say again.

"We did a good job," you say.

Now it is your turn. Think about a conflict you recently had with someone and reach a resolution.

Conflict definition

_____

_____

_____

_____

Problem resolution

_____

_____

_____

_____

CHAPTER 5

DBT COPING SKILLS TO MANAGE EMOTIONS AND AGGRESSIVE BEHAVIOR

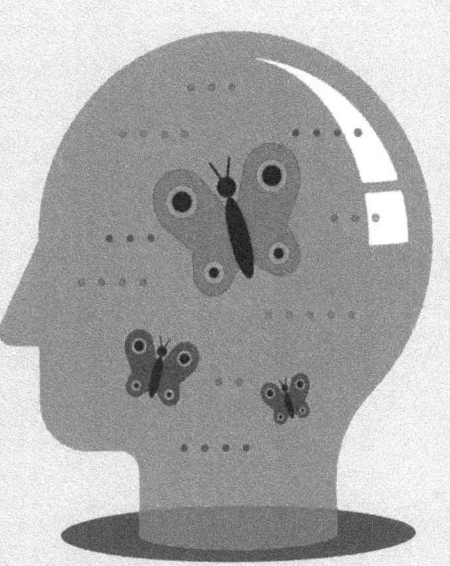

Kate's friend invited her to her home for a birthday party. Kate observed that as the celebration drew near, she had begun to worry about what the party would be like. Initially, she felt pleased to think of being there but then her mind kept wandering to the previous party she had attended, where some attendees had taunted her in front of her friends. Kate also observed that whenever she recalled those earlier incidents, she felt the anger, embarrassment, and shame again. Also, she began to get apprehensive about attending the party since she began to worry that it would be similar to the previous one.

She would occasionally begin to worry that something would go wrong again and that she would look silly, but as soon as she became aware of the anxiety and the thoughts that were causing it, she gave her full attention to what was occurring right then. She noticed she was feeling anxious. Her heart was pounding, and her palms were sweaty. She would then exhale profoundly and return her focus to whatever was happening.

At first, Kate discovered that she had to put a lot of effort into it, but as the evening wore on, she could unwind more time trying to focus on her wandering thoughts and simply understanding what was happening around her. She used DBT skills to manage her wandering thoughts.

You can also be present and enjoy your surroundings like Kate.

5.1. Introduction to DBT

DBT is an evidence-based therapy created by Marsha Linehan, at the University of Washington, to assist those who struggled with suicidal ideation, intense emotional swings, impulsivity, and interpersonal chaos.

The inability to successfully control and manage emotions in response to any imagined "prompting incident" limits the ability of many teens to grow and heal substantially. Any internal or external stimulus that causes emotion dysregulation is called a "prompting event."

An individual's life becomes meaningless and filled with hopelessness due to their inability to control their emotions. This will frequently cause disruption and frequently result in the breakdown of meaningful relationships, whether personal or professional. Many times, the person would have been able to successfully manage and regulate their emotions if they had been able to identify the prompting event and recognize the trigger.

The main objective of DBT skills is to help you build a supportive atmosphere in which you can regulate any emotional dysregulation.

Those who struggle to control their emotions, stress, relationships, and impulsive behaviors can benefit from dialectical behavior therapy (DBT). Cognitive behavioral therapy and mindfulness exercises are combined in DBT. DBT therapists use a sympathetic attitude, accepting you as you are while assisting you in making changes and achieving your objectives.

DBT's fundamental objective is to assist you in creating a worthwhile life.

Foundation of DBT

The foundation of DBT is the notion that opposites can thrive together. This entails accepting circumstances as they are, considering multiple points of view in every circumstance, and continuously juggling an effort to change.

You can benefit from DBT skills by learning how to:

- Deal with distress.
- Navigate through turbulent situations.
- Help in a crisis without exacerbating the situation.
- Understand and manage emotions.
- Ask for what they want or effectively say no.
- How to be in the present moment.

DBT Skills

Here are the basic DBT skills:

Mindfulness

The skill required for knowledge of reality and acceptance is mindfulness. It helps to be attentive to the present rather than the past or the future and be aware of what is inside and outside of you without passing judgment on what you are going through.

Distress Tolerance

Distance tolerance is the cornerstone of DBT. It encourages the development of acceptance of the present circumstance and crisis coping mechanisms to lessen the possibility of aggressive behavior, frequently making matters worse.

Emotional Regulation

Learning to recognize and categorize one's current emotions, recognizing barriers to emotional change, and lowering emotional reactivity are just a few of the abilities that can help support behavioral changes. These abilities are meant to make you less vulnerable and feel better.

Interpersonal Effectiveness

Interpersonal effectiveness is the collection of abilities that teaches practical methods for handling interpersonal conflict, saying no, and requesting what one wants.

The Stories of Different Minds

Being emotionally unstable or having trouble controlling your emotions causes you to respond to things in ways that most others wouldn't. You might feel more strongly and take longer to get back to your usual self. Your biology contributes to this emotion dysregulation, but that does not mean you cannot change it.

I will teach you three ways of thinking about things, some methods for slowing down the roller coaster so you can maintain some control, and some lifestyle decisions.

Your Wise Mind

Your Emotion Mind

Your Reasonable Mind

Three States of Mind

We all have three different modes of thought, or states of mind, according to DBT:

- The Reasonable Mind
- The Emotion Mind
- The Wise Mind

You must practice accessing these different states to improve your ability to manage your emotions. Of course, teens experiencing an emotional roller coaster tend to think about things more frequently than their emotional selves. We'll examine each mind in this section so you may practice becoming familiar with your mental states.

The Reasonable Mind

While you use your rational mind, you are thinking clearly and logically though solely considering the facts of the case. In this condition, emotions are typically absent or, if present, they are mild and have no bearing on your behavior. Examples include picking a college solely based on the degree programs it offers, the likelihood of getting a job after graduation, and the school's reputation rather than considering factors like how convenient it will be to visit home, whether you have friends who are currently enrolled there, and whether you like the way the campus looks and feels.

Everyday examples include doing your homework (as long as you are focused on it and aren't so angry with arithmetic that you hurl your book out the window!) and following your parents' instructions to get supper ready on a night when they'll both be arriving late.

If you frequently act against your best interests, you are probably not operating in a way that serves you, and this frequently results in emotional discomfort like anger. We want to concentrate on finding a middle ground between listening exclusively to your thinking and only to your emotions with this skill.

The Emotion Mind

Let's begin with the one you are most familiar with, your emotional self. Your behaviors are under the power of your emotions. If you are feeling anxious, you may also avoid the situation making you feel that way. For instance, you might skip class today to avoid having to give the presentation you were supposed to.

When you act based on your emotions, you are reacting rather than deciding. When you are in this mindset, you frequently act in ways you later regret, such as snapping at someone you care about or acting rashly with unfavorable long-term effects.

The Wise Mind

Your smart mind strikes a balance. It forces you to weigh both of these factors—your emotions and your reasoning—instead of making a binary decision. It also considers a third element, i.e., your gut instinct or intuition. You permit yourself to experience your emotions, and you consider what logic is telling you, but you also pay attention to that inner voice that has weighed the pros and cons of all the potential outcomes and is advising you on what will be most beneficial in the long run.

When was the last time your wise mind tried to attract your attention?

Although your ways pay attention to it, it exists. The thing your inner knowledge advises you to do is not always what's natural for you, it is what will ultimately be best for you, the circumstance, and other people.

Striking a Balance

You do not want to either be in yourself or only be in your logical self. This is another area where achieving balance in your life is essential. Both of these mental states are beneficial and necessary at different times. For instance, your emotional self includes pleasurable emotions like love, joy, and excitement, so you want to take advantage of those powerful feelings. But, the objective is to allow you to make better, healthier decisions by balancing your emotions with your thinking and bringing in your intuition.

5.2. Mindfulness

Since mindfulness enables you to become aware of your life, it is the foundational skill in DBT. Before you can alter anything, you must first become conscious of the truth about who you are, how you behave with others, how your actions affect others, and how you affect the world around you. Being present with your total concentration and acceptance is what mindfulness is all about.

It consists of two parts: accepting whatever you chance to find in this instant and focusing on what you are doing right now, in this very minute. As soon as you begin to practice mindfulness, you will notice that the world stops and that you become more conscious of your thoughts, bodily sensations, and emotional state. Also, you will be more interested in life and aware of what's happening around you.

Do you believe you give much thought to the past? It can be something that happened to you or in the distant past. Maybe it could be something more recently—like a fight or a test result. Consider for a second the feelings that typically surface. Anger? Resentment? Frustration? Regret? Sadness? Your mind may occasionally wander to positive recollections, such as the enjoyable time or the summer vacation you took with your family. However, most of the time, we revisit sad memories rather than happy ones.

You might be concerned about whether the girl you want will accept your invitation to the prom, whether you will seem foolish if you attend this weekend's huge party, and other things. Does this describe who you are? Again, sometimes we experience happy feelings when we ponder about the future.

There is more emotional suffering when you are not present. The present is only sometimes pleasant, of course. Because you are only dealing with it and not the agony of the past, present, and future simultaneously, even though there is a pain in the present, there is still less pain if you are more mindful.

The other component of mindfulness, acceptance, likewise lessens the emotional suffering you experience. Because of this, being more conscious makes you more tolerant, which reduces discomfort.

Mindfulness helps in:

- Raising positive feelings
- Lessening emotional suffering
- Being at ease and tranquil
- Enhancing self-control
- Enhancing memory
- Concentration
- Finding balance

How to Be Aware in Four Steps

Let's simplify things by breaking mindfulness down into manageable steps so you can understand how to apply mindfulness to every situation in your life.

Choose a Pastime

Pick an activity to concentrate on. Keep in mind that you may perform any activity attentively. When walking your dog, you can walk thoughtfully; if you are going to read, you might choose to read one page slowly.

Be Mindful

Concentrate on what you are reading as you immerse yourself in the narrative. You can focus on your surroundings, such as a squirrel darting across the road or the trees, or you can pay attention to how it physically feels to walk, such as how your feet feel on the pavement.

Take Note

Your mind will almost stray because our brain produces hundreds of thoughts daily. Recognize and note this.

Do not Pass judgment.

Refocus your attention on the present moment without passing judgment. This implies that you do not criticize your wandering or anything else that comes into your awareness, such as a particular thought that pops into your head or something you feel with your senses. Observe everything you chance to notice without passing judgment.

Now that you know how DBT can help you, let's go to the fun part and do some activities to apply what you have learned.

CHAPTER 6

DBT COPING SKILLS ACTIVITIES

Dialectical behavior therapy (DBT) will assist you in managing powerful emotions and behaviors. Coping skills, or techniques that teens can use to handle challenging emotions and behaviors, are essential skills taught in DBT. This chapter will pay particular attention to  coping mechanisms for controlling emotions, which you learned in the previous chapter, through exciting activities. By learning and using these skills, you can lessen your propensity to act out in dangerous or destructive ways.

6.1. Activity Corner

Let us learn and have some fun.

Activity 20: Identify Unmindful Thoughts

Read the stories listed below. Be aware that remaining in the past or the future is not healthy. It is likely to elicit more painful feelings.

Tell whether the following teens are mindful or unmindful (i.e., not present-focused and possibly passing judgment on the situation). Choose the term that is the most accurate.

1. William was quite upset and angry. He was confident that his friend Toby was discussing him with someone else. "I cannot believe Toby said those hurtful things," William reflected. This usually occurs to me; I'll never have trustworthy pals."

_____

_____

_____

2. Sandy's friends were conversing and enjoying themselves at a party. Sandy preferred to watch television by herself in the living room. She reflected, "I usually feel so uneasy at events while everyone else appears relaxed and comfortable. What's the matter with me? Why cannot I fit in."

_____

_____

_____

Activity 21: Identify Your Thinking Style

To help you determine your thinking style, check the boxes next to the statements you believe apply to you.

Reasonable Mind

The skill required for knowledge of reality and acceptance is mindfulness. It helps to be attentive to the present rather than the past or the future and be aware of what is inside and outside of you without passing judgment on what you are going through.

- ☐   I frequently make decisions despite my feelings.
- ☐   Usually, I have good motives behind what I do.
- ☐   I frequently have no idea what emotions I am experiencing.
- ☐   I feel more at ease discussing facts than emotions.

Emotion Mind

- ☐   I frequently give in to urges and say or do things I regret.
- ☐   I frequently find myself in stressful circumstances, making it difficult to think clearly.
- ☐   I frequently base my choices entirely on how I feel.
- ☐   After I've decided, I often second-guess it, wondering if I made the proper choice.

Wise Mind

- ☐   When I decide, I often weigh reasoning and feelings.
- ☐   I frequently feel at peace when I finally decide anything after deliberating for a time
- ☐   I feel safe letting myself experience my feelings.
- ☐   In the long run, I frequently behave in my best interests.

You may or may not fall primarily into one category after adding up your checkmarks for each one. You must begin to increase your awareness.

Which mind do you use?

Activity 22: Are You Judgmental?

We can make judgments in either a positive or negative way. We're more concerned with negative judgments because controlling your emotions is more challenging for you, so we're more interested in those. Practice recognizing when you are passing judgment favorably or unfavorably, though.

Read the following sentences carefully. Check the sentence to indicate if it is judgmental.

- ☐ My grade on the report card needed to be better.
- ☐ My folks have a nasty habit.
- ☐ I am a failure.
- ☐ When I let my rage out of control, I feel so frustrated with myself.
- ☐ It dramatically irritates me when my brother won't leave the computer when I need him to.
- ☐ I like my math subject this year but still need help with it.
- ☐ I do not believe posting images on social media is secure.

Activity 23: Need Some Changes

Think about the adjustments you want to make right now. You might begin implementing immediately to give you more control over your feelings.

The list of life aspects that can influence your emotions is provided below. Answer the inquiries in each part to ascertain whether this is a subject you ought to focus on;

Start putting those changes into practice.

Sleep

How many hours do you typically sleep each night?

_____

Do you typically wake up feeling rested?

_____

Do you typically feel tired after a nap?

_____

Considering your responses, you typically feel groggy and sluggish after sleeping; do you believe you need to lengthen or shorten your sleep cycles?

What is one tiny move you can take to improve this if you have decided it needs improvement?

(For instance, you can aim to go to bed 30 minutes earlier tonight to improve your sleep.)

(Start with a half-hour and work your way up.)

Eating

Do you consume three meals and a few snacks every day?

_____

Do you typically eat wholesome meals and snacks?

_____

Do you frequently overeat simply because you feel the want to do so?

_____

Is it out of boredom or a terrible emotion, like sadness?

_____

Do you often skip meals to reduce weight or feel better about yourself?

_____

People occasionally experience eating issues and need to seek help. If you believe you need improvement, talk to someone you trust.

What is one tiny step you can take to improve your diet?

_____

(For instance, cut sugar and fast food.)

Activity 24: Place Yourself on the Opposite Side

You might use this activity to reflect on instances in which you resisted your impulse and instances in which you could not do so. You can see what's working and what is not by reflecting on both the times you were able to act skillfully and the times you weren't and what you could do the next time. Please describe the mood you were feeling and the corresponding need. If you give in to the impulse, use the "no" route. If you refrain from acting on the urge, the "yes" path should be taken.

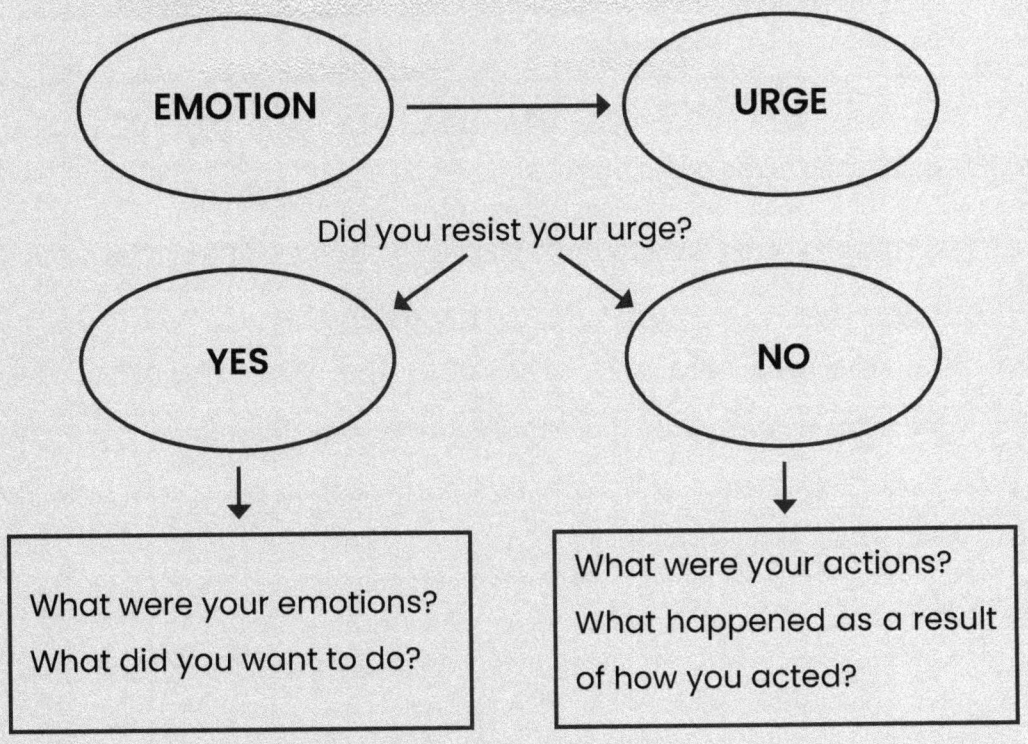

Activity 25: Self-validation

You will gain more experience with this exercise in recognizing your emotions and discovering several ways to talk to yourself about them. Example statements are below: You can say certain non-judgmental things to yourself.

- ☐ It is acceptable for me to feel this way.
- ☐ This human emotion is normal.
- ☐ Everyone experiences this at times.
- ☐ I feel this way for a reason.
- ☐ It is okay for me to feel this.

Try to think of more sentences in the area provided to assist you in thinking about these feelings in a non-judgmental, more reasonable manner.

_____

_____

_____

Activity 26: Prepare Your List of Activities

There are times in everyone's lives when their emotions get severe, and they do not know how to handle them. When this happens, we frequently want to do things that, while they may temporarily help us deal with our overwhelming emotions, ultimately harm us. You can learn healthy coping mechanisms from this activity, enabling you to get through a crisis. Checkmark the activities you want to do, make your own list on a separate piece of paper to carry with you, and refer to it as a means of self-distraction in times of need.

- ☐ Doodle, paint, or make art.
- ☐ Examine pictures.
- ☐ Compose a poem or a narrative.
- ☐ Consider instances in which you felt joy.
- ☐ Dance or sing.
- ☐ Examine previous yearbooks.
- ☐ Envision your future after graduation.
- ☐ Spend some time outside.
- ☐ Mention the positive aspects of your personality.
- ☐ Watch your preferred TV show or movie.
- ☐ Go somewhere and observe people.
- ☐ Message someone you miss.
- ☐ Play some music for relaxation.
- ☐ Spend some time with a pal.
- ☐ Try out a variety of hairstyles.
- ☐ Shut your eyes and travel to your favorite location in your mind.
- ☐ Journal.
- ☐ Play a sport that you like.

Your list

_____

_____

_____

_____

Activity 27: Write it Down

Fill this sheet and plan to follow when in crisis.

My Triggers

_____

_____

_____

My Warning Sign (When you are losing control)

_____

_____

_____

I can sooth myself with

_____

_____

My support system (name some people who you can trust in times of crisis)

_____

_____

_____

Activity 28: Be Productive

List any hobbies you believe will make you feel good about yourself in the following box. For a place to start, consider these:

- Helping someone in need
- Achieving a high math grade.
- Sweeping the driveway of my neighbor
- Completing my responsibilities on time

If you are having trouble coming up with something that will make you feel proud or accomplished, try thinking positively about yourself. What advice would you provide to a buddy attempting to develop ways to boost her self-esteem? Remember that you can always seek a reliable person for assistance.

_____

_____

_____

Activity 29: Box Breathing

Box breathing will assist you in relaxing your nervous system.

Deep breathing supports the body's ability to do a variety of things, including:

- Relax and regulate the nervous system.
- Help the body deal with stress.
- Ease worry
- Get more oxygen into the body.

Use 5 seconds timeline on each side of the box. Your body will feel calm and comfortable after this activity.

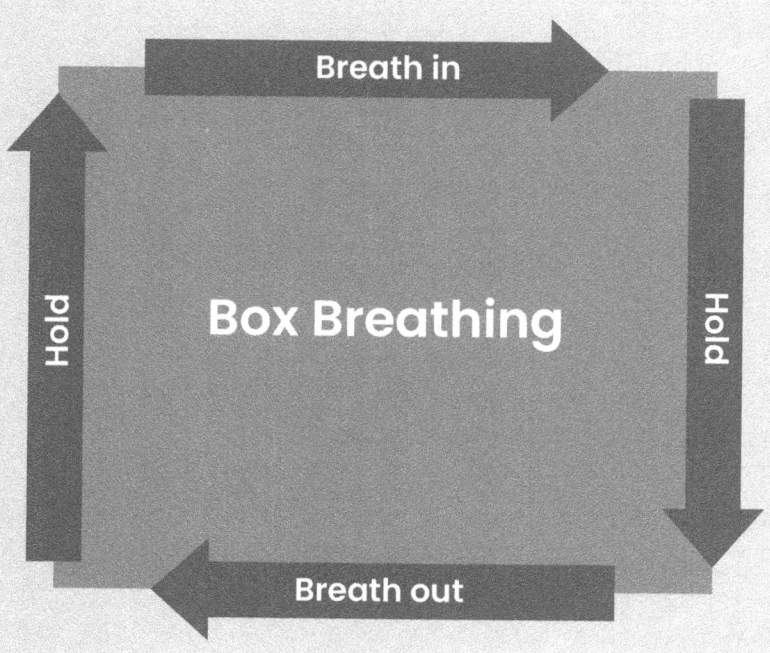

Breath in

Hold

Box Breathing

Hold

Breath out

Activity 30: Let Them Flow

Let your emotions and feeling flow.

Close your eyes while seated or lying down. Imagine yourself in a river in your head. Your knees are submerged, and a light current brush against your legs. You will notice how your thoughts and feelings slowly float by you as the current carries them downstream. Observe them as they  pass rather than attempting to grab onto them or become entangled in them.

Come back to simply standing river if you become preoccupied with a concept or an emotion to the point where you are riding it instead of observing it float by. Redirect your focus to the practice and concentrate on simply watching. As much as you can, do not pass judgment on the ideas or emotions that come and go; acknowledge their existence.

Activity 31: Your Positive Diary

The way you feel, influences how you perceive about the world. Happier feelings allow you to recognize the significant aspects of your life.

When you are depressed, you tend to concentrate on the bad. Despite how you are feeling, the goal of this exercise is to remove those blinders and put more of your attention on the good things in your life.

Fill out the accompanying worksheet for the next two weeks, noting at least one encouraging development each day and your feelings and thoughts around it. It might be a sensation you have, something kind someone does or says to you (or something kind you do or says to someone else!), a stunning sunrise, a good grade you get in school, or a calm, relaxing moment you have while you sit in the sunshine. Whatever it is, what matters is that you are aware of it as it is happening.

Date	Positive and happy events	How did you feel?

Activity 32: Apply What You Learned

Choose a scenario that is likely to occur in the future, such as being asked to do something you do not want to do or learning about a party you still need to inform your parents about. Put it here in writing:

_____

_____

How would you assert yourself in this circumstance?

_____

_____

Return to this workbook after having this discussion. Did you behave firmly? What happened as a result?

_____

_____

Were you pleased with the results? Were there any actions you could have taken to produce a better result?

_____

_____

CHAPTER 7

IMPROVING
YOUR
RELATIONSHIPS

When Rose and Sophia initially met, their friendship grew stronger with time. Yet, in the coming years, Rose began to observe a change in her friend's behavior. Sophia didn't appear to care as much about their friendship as she once did, and Rose began to feel irrelevant to her friend. They had both made some new friends. Rose remained silent out of fear of upsetting Sophia, and her hurt grew. Rose started to feel resentful of how much effort she was putting in.

Rose decided to relieve Sophia of her commitment one day because she had had enough of feeling as if she owed her more than ever. Rose informed Sophia that it was finished between them and both of them would need to find their path. The two got into a heated argument. Both said cruel things and were put in the difficult situation of trying to coexist amid the uncomfortable and tense situation. The relationship had ended.

Have any of your relationships ever ended this way? Instead of taking action that might help save the connection, people frequently let relationships end even though they do not want it to happen. Remember that if you want your relationships to continue, you must care for them. If you ignore them or allow your emotions to get in the way of your behavior, you can count on the connection ending somehow.

The relationships you have in your life—with family, friends, romantic interests, teachers, or coaches, among others—will also impact your mood and your capacity for managing your emotions. Surviving it undoubtedly has a lot to do with learning techniques to help you do so.

Your surroundings significantly impact how you feel, how fulfilling and healthy your relationships are, and how they impact your mood and how you feel about yourself. Hence, in this chapter, we'll examine the importance of relationships in more detail. You will be asked to consider the connections you presently have in your life, their level of satisfaction and health.

7.1. Importance of Building Relationships

You should have a lot of relationships with whom you feel comfortable discussing your life's private things. There are some people with whom you interact but do not discuss private matters, yet you enjoy spending time with them.

on the other hand, there are some people with whom you discuss your private matters. There is not any comprehensive list; the objective is to get you to have more relationships.

Why is this crucial?

If you do not have many pals, you will need to rely on the people in your life, which is your family. This circumstance has the potential to be quite emotionally painful. For instance, how do you phone your only buddy to set up plans, but she claims she's already booked? And it can be detrimental to those on whom you have grown dependent. If you depend on just one person, your relationships will not be healthier. Your friend cannot spend all of their time with you.

Have you ever observed moments where certain people start acting differently? This is typically a hint to take a break.

What do you do when one person takes a family vacation? Or becomes ill? Who will you turn to if someone is not available?

Please understand me: I am not suggesting you cannot be independent and that you need other people to support you through every difficulty. But for us as humans, relationships with other people are crucial.

Being alone has detrimental effects on not only our bodies but also our emotional wellness.

- Do you have a sufficient number of friends and family?
- Do you possess folks with whom you can socialize and have fun?
- Do you have relationships that will support you and on whom you can rely?
- Do you know anyone with whom you can talk to, even if you do not disclose your most private matters to them?

Think from your wise self, and speak honestly about this.

We'll discuss this if you do not have it in your life.

But for now, let's start with what you already have.

Consider how to maintain the relationships that are already present in your life. Maintaining your relationships is crucial if you want to prevent a breakdown. Consider a relationship as you would do a car. You must take care of significant problems, such as an engine rattle when they occur, but maintaining your vehicle, such as changing the oil and rotating the tires, can frequently stop those more significant issues from developing. The more tenderly you handle, the more frequently you maintain your relationships.

7.2. Activity Corner

Let's learn some techniques to improve your relationships by doing some fun activities.

Activity 33: Get in Touch with Past Relationships

First consider the relationships you once had with people who are no longer close friends with you for any reason. Write their names:

_____

_____

Plan how you would contact that individual if you needed to. Jot down some ideas for how to contact them:

_____

_____

Consider what you would say if you get in touch with this person. Do you need to set the record straight on something that occurred between you, for instance? Think about what you would say and then write it down:

_____

_____

Remember that, especially in the beginning, the relationship probably won't be the same as it formerly was; friendships need time to grow, so be patient.

Activity 34: Meeting New People

Can you come up with multiple ways to meet new people?

Add your thoughts to these examples:

Join a new club at your school.

Enroll in foreign language classes.

Become active with a local youth organization.

Volunteer at an animal shelter or food bank.

Sign up for a school sport.

_____

_____

_____

_____

Going out to people can be incredibly scary for many of us. Yet remember that relationships are a vital aspect of life. If doing this alone makes you anxious, think about doing it with a friend. You may have a buddy going through something similar, and you two can concentrate on improving your relationships.

Thinking back to when you had more relationships—someone you could call to speak about issues, people you could contact to hang out—can also be beneficial.

Can you still recall how it felt to be loved, accepted by others, and welcomed? People are social creatures, and we require relationships throughout our life. Therefore, you must discover ways to meet this demand.

Activity 35: Constructive Communication Worksheet

Communication Styles

We all have a particular communication style. So, it is essential to recognize your communication style. First, you need to know these types and identify your style. Only then can we change it?

Put checks next to the appropriate questions as you consider each to express yourself best. Once you are done, total the number of checkmarks to determine which forms of communication you employ most frequently in each segment.

Passive Communication

- ☐ I try to push away folks instead of expressing my emotions to them.
- ☐ I'm afraid that if I speak up, people will be angry with me.
- ☐ I frequently catch myself saying, "I do not care" or "That does not matter to me."
- ☐ I try to remain silent in order to "avoid rocking the boat."
- ☐ I frequently share their opinions, but I try not to insult anyone.

Your score:

Aggressive Communication

- ☐ I'm concerned with getting my way, regardless of how it impacts other people.
- ☐ I frequently yell, swear, or use other harsh verbal expressions.
- ☐ My friends are pretty afraid of me.
- ☐ Some have said that I have a "I will do it my way" mentality.

Your score:

Passive-Aggressive Communication

- ☐ I often use caustic language when conversing with other people.
- ☐ I frequently treat people silently when I'm angry with them.
- ☐ It is pretty usual for me to say one thing while really thinking another.
- ☐ I usually turn to violent actions, like slamming doors, rather than using words to express my emotions.
- ☐ I try to communicate my ideas more quietly.
- ☐ People will get angry with me or stop loving me if I express myself.

Your score:

Assertive Communication

- [ ] I absolutely believe that I have the right to express my opinions.
- [ ] I have the ability to express my disagreement with someone.
- [ ] I am capable of expressing myself openly and honestly.
- [ ] I treat people with respect when I talk to them.
- [ ] I listen carefully to what others have to say.
- [ ] I'm trying to understand their perspective.
- [ ] If our goals are at odds, I strive to find a compromise.

Your score:

It is critical to recognize your style so you can improve them.

Please read the following tips to succeed in having an assertive style; it is worth your time.

Here are some precise strategies to make you good at communicating your concerns. Prepare notes on your performance with each strategy in the area provided:

Be specific about your goals. Do you communicate openly and truthfully?

_____

_____

Pay attention as you listen. Do you ignore everything else and concentrate only on who you are conversing with?

_____

_____

Be without bias. Do you try to avoid passing judgment, placing blame, and keeping your opinions and facts to yourself?

_____

_____

Affirm others. Do you ask questions in response to what someone is saying?

_____

_____

Follow your morals and values when acting. Do you try to act honestly?

_____

_____

Do not apologize too much. Do you frequently catch yourself apologizing for something?

_____

_____

7.3. Designing a Plan

You will gradually develop healthier emotional management skills. In this last section, I'll give you some suggestions about how to go forward. You must finish the job you have begun to bring about those beneficial improvements.

Spend some time first considering what you could change to benefit. For instance, you might have to make your way through rereading this book slowly and honing your abilities more each time as you proceed. Occasionally, readers speed through specific information without exerting the maximum effort possible. The outcome is that they need to properly absorb the information to orate their lives with the knowledge.

Reading this book too soon can also lead to the experience of learning so much that you start feeling overwhelmed. So, go about it step by step. Take your time, even if it means concentrating on one skill for a few months.

You must act to understand the subject and produce beneficial and healthy decisions.

Writing down a plan can help with this, as it can with most of the things in life. You may write down some thoughts on this on a blank paper.

Have you recently started a mindfulness practice, for instance?

Have you been more aware of when your emotions or wise self-governs you?

Have you been attempting to speak more efficiently with others to strengthen your bonds with them?

What is keeping you from completing the task?

Do you know if these skills will be beneficial?

Remind yourself that if such ideas are preventing you from moving forward. You must change your approach. Try to find a means to go past it. Ask friends and relatives for assistance if you cannot do it alone. Spend some time reading through this book's chapters. Focus on improving self-calming activities.

Try to find a skill that will be challenging for you. Consider this as the place you should start with.

Supporting Yourself!

Remember that the thoughts and words you choose to describe your emotions and actions have a huge impact. Pay attention to how you speak about the efforts you are attempting. When you fail to meet a goal, encourage yourself. Perhaps even a compilation of motivating self-talks that you might read aloud to yourself while you are having a hard time would work, for instance, "This is terrible, but as I keep going, I'll succeed."

Seeking Assistance

Asking for assistance does not indicate weakness; on the contrary, it takes guts. Be glad you are attempting to assist yourself while thinking of them. Improve your emotional control. The activities given in this chapter will benefit those who care well. Nonetheless, remember that if you request assistance, you must be prepared to accept the assistance provided—thus try not to resent your family or friends and act from your knowledgeable self.

Final Thoughts

When you have trouble controlling your emotions, you discover that life frequently feels overwhelming. Both your self-esteem and your relationships suffer. It might be challenging to achieve goals, do well in school, and think clearly. The knowledge you have gained from this book will help you to regulate your emotions.

You have noticed specific achievements if you have diligently put them into action, though they could only be minor. Yet, it will be more advantageous as you continue using these abilities over time.

You will notice changes.

Of course, it is challenging, and you must fully adopt the new perspective. Just reading this book will not help you make changes; you must use the techniques and put effort towards altering how you have been living. Perseverance in developing abilities is the key.

It takes time to adjust how you deal (or do not deal!) with your emotions. You must remember that you have been trapped in this habit all your life. It will be possible for you to wait to make these modifications.

You should eventually see favorable change if you work hard to develop these skills. Everyone experiences changes differently, and everyone is different. If you put in the effort, you can make a happier, healthier version of yourself. I hope your adventure is successful.

After Reading This Book Give Your Honest Review

www.ingramcontent.com/pod-product-compliance
Lightning Source LLC
Chambersburg PA
CBHW041517120626
46551CB00018B/2469